Puzzle Time!

LARGE PRINT PUZZLES CROSSWORDS

igloobooks

igloobooks

Published in 2018
by Igloo Books Ltd
Cottage Farm
Sywell
NN6 0BJ
www.igloobooks.com

VIV001 1217
2 4 6 8 10 9 7 5 3
ISBN 978-1-78670-911-0

Cover designed by Nicholas Gage

Puzzle compilation, typesetting and design by:
Clarity Media Ltd, http://www.clarity-media.co.uk

Printed and manufactured in Malaysia

Contents

No. 1

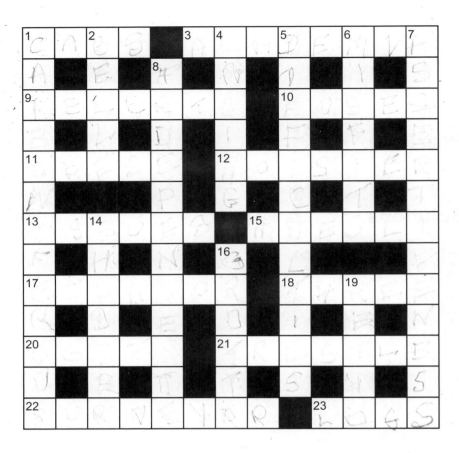

Across

1 Taxis (4)
3 The scholastic world (8)
9 Becomes less severe (7)
10 Combines (5)
11 Corpulent (5)
12 Less quiet (7)
13 Topics for debate (6)
15 Breakfast food (6)
17 Republic in South America (7)
18 Number in a trio (5)
20 ___ Nash: writer of light verse (5)
21 Table support (7)
22 Building examiner (8)
23 Official records (4)

Down

1 Period of the Palaeozoic era (13)
2 Attractive young lady (5)
4 Housing (6)
5 Tricky elements; obstacles (12)
6 Outsiders (7)
7 Aggressive self-assurance (13)
8 Freedom from control (12)
14 Quiver (7)
16 Small cave (6)
19 Quantitative relation (5)

No. 2

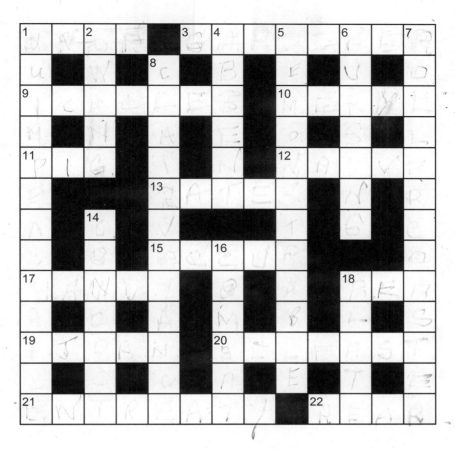

Across

1 On top of (4)
3 Horticulturist (8)
9 Frozen water spears (7)
10 ___ Streep: Mamma Mia! actress (5)
11 Hog (3)
12 Foolishly credulous (5)
13 Assesses performance (5)
15 Take place (5)
17 Useful (5)
18 Small legume (3)
19 ___ Ulvaeus: member of ABBA (5)
20 Capital of Northern Ireland (7)
21 Supplication (8)
22 Hind part (4)

Down

1 Totally trustworthy (13)
2 Outstanding (of a debt) (5)
4 Not present (6)
5 Clearly evident (12)
6 Caring for (7)
7 Amusement park ride (6,7)
8 Ability to see the future (12)
14 Make by mixing ingredients (7)
16 Fighting between armed forces (6)
18 Shallow circular dish (5)

No. 3

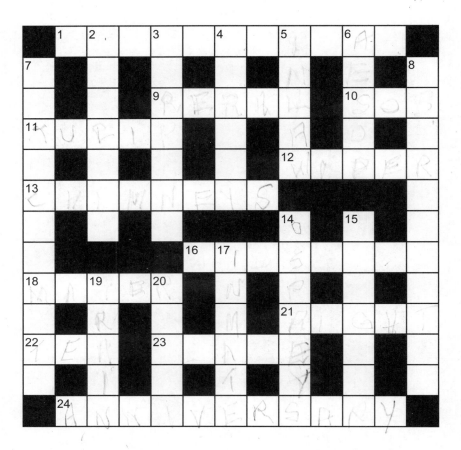

Across

1 Re-evaluation (11)
9 Danger (5)
10 Cry (3)
11 Spring flower (5)
12 Device that clears a car windscreen (5)
13 Vertical flues (8)
16 US state (8)
18 Female parent (5)
21 Correct (5)
22 Ate (anag) (3)
23 Stop (5)
24 Yearly celebration (11)

Down

2 Notable feat (7)
3 Bursting (7)
4 Scarcity (6)
5 Relation by marriage (2-3)
6 Greek writer of fables (5)
7 Small room that leads to a main one (11)
8 Shortened (11)
14 Fish-eating birds of prey (7)
15 Thief (7)
17 Prisoner (6)
19 Instruct; teach (5)
20 Christina ___ : actress (5)

No. 4

Across

1 Baby beds (4)
3 Conceited (8)
9 Chats (7)
10 Borders (5)
11 Send money (5)
12 Assign (7)
13 Most secure (6)
15 Make a bubbling sound (6)
17 Dowager (anag) (7)
18 Spends time doing nothing (5)
20 Roger ___ : English actor (5)
21 Procedure; standard (7)
22 Opposite of positive (8)
23 Fitness centres (4)

Down

1 Female politician in the US (13)
2 ___ pole: tribal emblem (5)
4 Scoundrel (6)
5 Unnecessarily careful (12)
6 Fishing (7)
7 Blandness (13)
8 Second part of the Bible (3,9)
14 220 yards (7)
16 History play by Shakespeare (5,1)
19 People not ordained (5)

No. 5

Across

1 Sweet potatoes (4)
3 Boastful person (8)
9 A Roman Catholic devotion (7)
10 Bedfordshire town (5)
11 Hostility (12)
13 Hold a position or job (6)
15 Taxonomic groupings (6)
17 Myopic (5-7)
20 Sign of the zodiac (5)
21 Imprecise (7)
22 Qualified for by right (8)
23 Extras (cricket) (4)

Down

1 Annual (8)
2 Tycoon (5)
4 Took it easy (6)
5 Birds of prey (6,6)
6 Prompting device (7)
7 Musical or vocal sound (4)
8 Crucial (3,9)
12 Official orders (8)
14 Live together (7)
16 Aim to achieve something (6)
18 Sycophant (5)
19 Merriment (4)

Across

1 Eg from Tokyo (8)
5 Sea inlet (4)
8 Pulls along forcefully (5)
9 Daydream (7)
10 Fled from captivity (7)
12 Pragmatist (7)
14 Seats for more than one person (7)
16 Brushed off the face (of hair) (7)
18 Eagerness (7)
19 Male relation (5)
20 Corner (4)
21 Great adulation (8)

Down

1 Popular martial art (4)
2 Public square in Italy (6)
3 Capital of Tennessee (9)
4 Thoroughfare (6)
6 Not ready to eat (of fruit) (6)
7 Liberties (8)
11 Without interruption (9)
12 Control (8)
13 Requesting (6)
14 Steady (anag) (6)
15 Evoke (6)
17 Declare untrue (4)

No. 7

Across

1 Beer and lemonade drink (6)
5 ___ Hanks: US actor (3)
7 Animal used for riding (5)
8 Spend lavishly (7)
9 Opposite of old (5)
10 Treat with drugs (8)
12 Shun (6)
14 Maiden (6)
17 Precious metallic element (8)
18 Stroll (5)
20 Solid inorganic substance (7)
21 Faint bird cry (5)
22 Long-haired ox (3)
23 Loves dearly (6)

Down

2 Occurs (7)
3 Controlled; managed (8)
4 Dull colour (4)
5 Insubstantial (7)
6 Non-pedigree dog (7)
7 SI unit of frequency (5)
11 ___ down the hatches: prepared for a crisis (8)
12 To the same degree (7)
13 Prune (3,4)
15 Imitate (7)
16 Decline sharply (5)
19 Not odd (4)

Across

1 Urges to act (6)
7 Pharmacists (8)
8 Towards the stern (3)
9 Long-legged rodent (6)
10 Fancy (4)
11 Headgear of a monarch (5)
13 Sickness (7)
15 Progress (7)
17 Famous English racetrack (5)
21 Very short skirt or dress (4)
22 Martial art (4,2)
23 Label (3)
24 Large marsupial (8)
25 Quality in speech arousing pity (6)

Down

1 Sloping (of a typeface) (6)
2 Edible plant tuber (6)
3 Set piece in rugby (5)
4 Readable (7)
5 Sightings (8)
6 Colours glass or wood (6)
12 Marriages (8)
14 Large ships (7)
16 ___ Wood: US actor (6)
18 Clasp (6)
19 Colours slightly (6)
20 Spy (5)

Across

1 Flower-shaped competition awards (8)
5 US state (4)
8 Charming and endearing (5)
9 Hinged surface on an aeroplane wing (7)
10 Tidal mouth of a river (7)
12 Marched (7)
14 Loud enough to be heard (7)
16 Freshness (7)
18 Shaving of the crown of head (7)
19 Damp (5)
20 Plant of the pea family (4)
21 Of striking beauty (8)

Down

1 Rough or harsh sound (4)
2 Dual audio (6)
3 Carved and painted post (5,4)
4 Avoided (6)
6 Imminent danger (6)
7 Social insect (8)
11 Workman; shopkeeper (9)
12 Ringing in the ears (8)
13 Ostentatiously showy (6)
14 Feature (6)
15 Swimming costume (6)
17 Adult male deer (4)

No. 10

Across
1 Military force (4)
3 Oversight (8)
9 The Pope (7)
10 Plant spike (5)
11 Make law (5)
12 A precise point in time (7)
13 Exertion (6)
15 Notable inconvenience (6)
17 Choice cut of beef (7)
18 Domesticated (5)
20 Birds' bills (5)
21 Relating to Oxford (7)
22 Commonplace (8)
23 ___ of Wight: largest island of England (4)

Down
1 Capable of being understood (13)
2 Obsession (5)
4 Small cake (6)
5 Contentment (12)
6 Lines of equal pressure on maps (7)
7 Absence (13)
8 Triumphantly (12)
14 Hot fire (7)
16 Long-haired variety of cat (6)
19 Female servants (5)

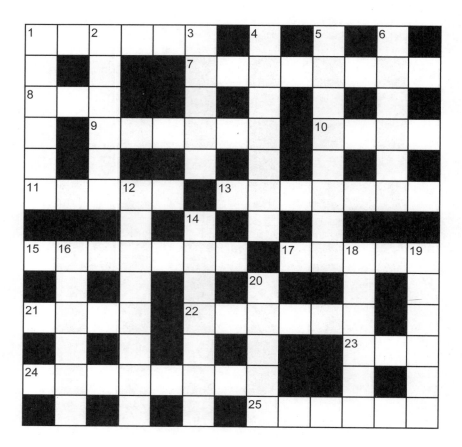

Across

1 Rides a bike (6)
7 Strongholds (8)
8 Make imperfect (3)
9 Unidirectional (3-3)
10 Large holes in the ground (4)
11 Resay (anag) (5)
13 Banners or flags (7)
15 Gets away (7)
17 Leg joints (5)
21 River sediment (4)
22 Cricket statistician (6)
23 Pub (3)
24 Expression of gratitude (5,3)
25 Entreated; beseeched (6)

Down

1 Conform (6)
2 Gaseous envelope of the sun (6)
3 Unpleasant facial expression (5)
4 Remaining (7)
5 Take up of a practice (8)
6 Substance present in cereal grains (6)
12 Cooking in the oven (8)
14 Jumpers (7)
16 Small in degree (6)
18 Weirdly (6)
19 Autographed something for a fan (6)
20 Appear suddenly (3,2)

Across

1 Freedom from difficulty (4)
3 Notes; sees (8)
9 A general proposition (7)
10 Animal life of a region (5)
11 Extent or limit (5)
12 Terrestrial (7)
13 Area with coin-operated games (6)
15 Magnitude (6)
17 Make ineffective (7)
18 Remain very close to (5)
20 Join together; merge (5)
21 Plants that live a year or less (7)
22 Beat out grain (8)
23 Settlement smaller than a city (4)

Down

1 Amusement (13)
2 Harsh and serious in manner (5)
4 Exceptionally large or successful (6)
5 Bubbling (12)
6 Coupon (7)
7 Black Eyed Peas star (5,8)
8 Amiability (12)
14 Coal miner (7)
16 Revolve quickly (6)
19 US state (5)

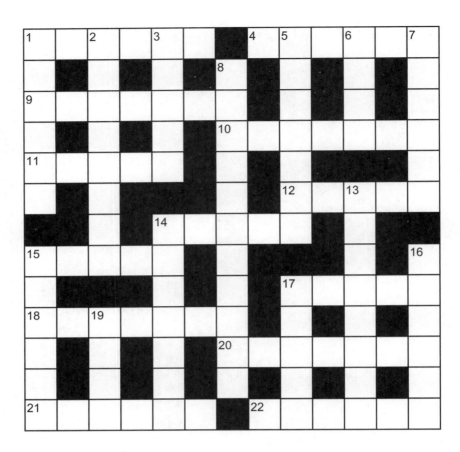

Across

1 Make unhappy (6)
4 Change over (6)
9 Schematic (7)
10 Unlawful (7)
11 ___ on : encouraged (5)
12 Grooved ring (5)
14 Coarse rock used for polishing (5)
15 Tines (anag) (5)
17 More pleasant (5)
18 Heart-shaped (7)
20 Serviettes (7)
21 Without difficulty (6)
22 Piece of text that names the writer of an article (6)

Down

1 Abrupt (6)
2 Game played on a chessboard (8)
3 Made a mistake (5)
5 Marsupial (7)
6 Mineral powder (4)
7 Inn (6)
8 Small pieces (11)
13 Courgette (US) (8)
14 Type of alcohol (7)
15 Provoke (6)
16 Robinson ___ : novel (6)
17 Crisp; pleasantly cold (5)
19 Fixes the result (4)

Across

1 Division of a group (6)
5 Witch (3)
7 Brief appearance (5)
8 Raging fire (7)
9 Metal spikes (5)
10 Manual of instruction (8)
12 Harry ___ : One Direction singer (6)
14 Hurt or troubled (6)
17 Made (a noise) less intense (8)
18 Breathing organs of fish (5)
20 Rush around in a violent manner (7)
21 Married women (5)
22 Eg oxygen (3)
23 Edits (6)

Down

2 Satisfied (7)
3 Cleansed thoroughly (8)
4 Portent (4)
5 On the ___ : about to happen (7)
6 Understood; held (7)
7 Chocolate powder (5)
11 Spice (8)
12 Making melodious sounds (7)
13 Eg primrose and lemon (7)
15 Came into view (7)
16 Bares (anag) (5)
19 Rescue (4)

Across

1 Step down from a job (6)
4 Sear (6)
9 Sully (7)
10 Charged with a crime (7)
11 Administrative capital of Bolivia (2,3)
12 Variety show (5)
14 Water container (5)
15 Devout (5)
17 Sum; add up (5)
18 Harmonious relationship (7)
20 Annoying (7)
21 Pass by (6)
22 Chant; speak solemnly (6)

Down

1 Narrate a story once again (6)
2 ___ for cash: short of money (8)
3 Ostentatious glamour (5)
5 Worry (7)
6 Flows (4)
7 Manage; hold (6)
8 Very charming (11)
13 Person highly skilled in music (8)
14 Past events (7)
15 Belt worn round the waist (6)
16 Sheepskin (6)
17 Spoken for (5)
19 Earnest appeal (4)

No. 16

Across

1 Opposite of least (4)
3 Sheath for a sword (8)
9 Uppermost layer of something (7)
10 Baking appliances (5)
11 Scientific research rooms (12)
13 Possibility (6)
15 Musical works (6)
17 Insubordination (12)
20 Dislikes intensely (5)
21 Sideways looks (7)
22 Fretting (8)
23 Rode (anag) (4)

Down

1 Lose (8)
2 Small woody plant (5)
4 Large strong boxes (6)
5 Pertaining to a person's life (12)
6 Eternal (7)
7 Piece of office furniture (4)
8 Unpredictably (12)
12 Evaluator (8)
14 Pilot (7)
16 Ronald ___ : former US President (6)
18 Tortilla topped with cheese (5)
19 Display (4)

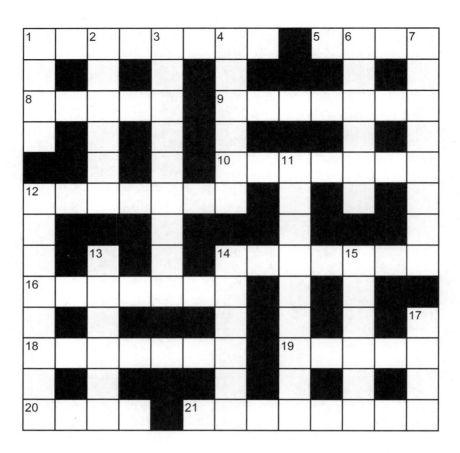

Across

1 Song for several voices (8)
5 Black ___: Colombian bird (4)
8 Angry (5)
9 Time off (7)
10 Countries (7)
12 Dressing (7)
14 Toxin in the body (7)
16 ___ Crowe: Gladiator actor (7)
18 Reluctance to change (7)
19 State indirectly (5)
20 Obtains (4)
21 Become part of a solution (8)

Down

1 Letters and parcels generally (4)
2 Deprive of force; stifle (6)
3 Intoxicate (9)
4 In poor health (6)
6 Nerve cell (6)
7 Strong dislike (8)
11 Gives evidence in court (9)
12 Getting onto a ship (8)
13 Agreement (6)
14 Opposite of an acid (6)
15 Thing that is totally true (6)
17 Computer memory unit (4)

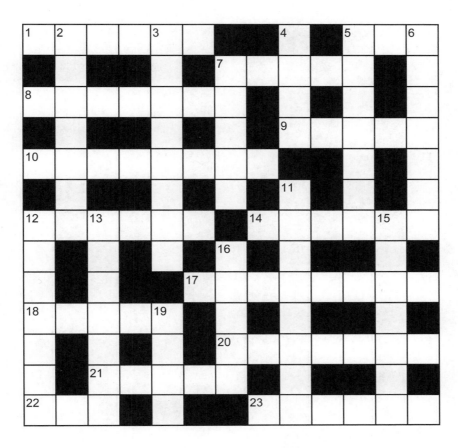

Across

1 Person who copies out documents (6)
5 Wager (3)
7 Search rigorously for (5)
8 Coat; decorate lavishly (7)
9 Rescuer (5)
10 Policemen or women (8)
12 Very cold (6)
14 Nimble (6)
17 Plummet (8)
18 Asserts; affirms (5)
20 Early 20th century art movement (7)
21 Warming drink (5)
22 Long-leaved lettuce (3)
23 Decorate with a raised design (6)

Down

2 Needle-leaved tree (7)
3 Reliable stock market company (4,4)
4 Tennis shots (4)
5 Boastful behaviour (7)
6 Holiday visitor (7)
7 Violent weather (5)
11 Item of additional book matter (8)
12 Extreme enthusiast (7)
13 Ten sirs (anag) (7)
15 Puts money into a venture (7)
16 Sullen; morose (5)
19 Soft drink (US) (4)

Across

1 Young deer (4)
3 Canine that herds animals (8)
9 Attains (7)
10 Push back (5)
11 Fantastical creature (3)
12 Lying flat (5)
13 Kick out (5)
15 Praise highly (5)
17 ___ Lewis: British singer (5)
18 Position of employment (3)
19 Break out with force (5)
20 Regeneration (7)
21 Delays it (anag) (8)
22 Primary colour (4)

Down

1 Absent-mindedness (13)
2 Fixed platform by water (5)
4 Bushy plant of the mint family (6)
5 Excessively loud (12)
6 Brings to effective action (7)
7 50th anniversary of a major event (6,7)
8 Showing complete commitment (12)
14 Sense of resolution (7)
16 Relating to stars (6)
18 Precious stone (5)

Across

1 Eg beef or pork (4)
3 Section of a train (8)
9 Frog larva (7)
10 Small fruit used for oil (5)
11 Country whose capital is Valletta (5)
12 Act of awakening from sleep (7)
13 Excessively ornate (of music) (6)
15 Rents out (6)
17 Low evergreen plant (7)
18 One of the United Arab Emirates (5)
20 Reel for winding yarn (5)
21 Travelling very quickly (7)
22 Rigidly; sternly (8)
23 In a lazy way (4)

Down

1 Process of transformation (of an insect) (13)
2 Paula ___ : US singer (5)
4 Stadiums (6)
5 Evergreen shrub (12)
6 Assumed identities (7)
7 Eternally (13)
8 Not intoxicating (of a drink) (12)
14 Utter noisily (7)
16 Largest South American country (6)
19 Impossible to see round (of a bend) (5)

No. 21

Across

1 Change in appearance (11)
9 Wireless (5)
10 One and one (3)
11 ___ Schmidt: film starring Jack Nicholson (5)
12 Long pointed elephant teeth (5)
13 Drink (8)
16 Metrical analysis of verse (8)
18 Snarl (5)
21 Earthy pigment (5)
22 Male offspring (3)
23 Rivulet (5)
24 Multiply (11)

Down

2 Decide firmly (7)
3 Bring up (7)
4 Growing dimmer (6)
5 Phantasm (5)
6 Religious acts (5)
7 Astound (11)
8 Shipment (11)
14 Cue sport (7)
15 Lacking; not having (7)
17 Designated limit (3,3)
19 Possessor (5)
20 Published false statement (5)

No. 22

Across

1 Intense feeling of love (6)
4 Female monster (6)
9 Sports arena (7)
10 Rattish (anag) (7)
11 Spacious (5)
12 Loathe (5)
14 Well-known (5)
15 Strong lightweight wood (5)
17 Gave away (5)
18 Enticed (7)
20 Tallest species of penguin (7)
21 Surprise results (6)
22 Privileged and well off (6)

Down

1 Soak up (6)
2 Line joining corners of a square (8)
3 Oneness (5)
5 Deity (7)
6 At any time (4)
7 Person gliding on ice (6)
8 Petty (5-6)
13 Hampered (8)
14 Most obese (7)
15 Flat-bottomed rowing boat (6)
16 Worshipped (6)
17 Island in the Bay of Naples (5)
19 Wipes up (4)

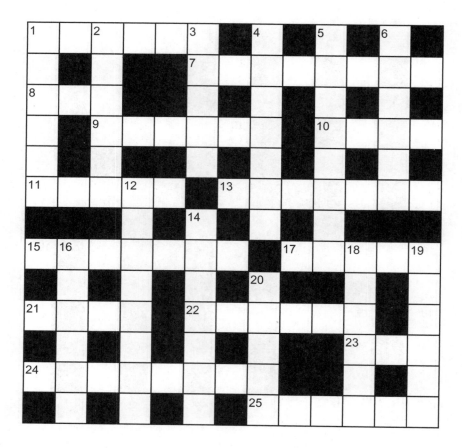

Across
1 Quickly (6)
7 Irresponsible (8)
8 Title of a married woman (3)
9 Make beloved (6)
10 US pop star who sang I Got You Babe (4)
11 Sticky sap (5)
13 Female inheritor (7)
15 Divisions between groups of people (7)
17 Arm of a body of water (5)
21 Not in favour (4)
22 Hurting (6)
23 Ancient pot (3)
24 Design engraved into a material (8)
25 Part of a cannon behind the bore (6)

Down
1 Treat with excessive indulgence (6)
2 Be preoccupied with (6)
3 Make available for sale (5)
4 Flee (7)
5 Elementary negatively charged particle (8)
6 Steers (anag) (6)
12 Harmful in effect (8)
14 Affably (7)
16 Written rules for church policy (6)
18 Bean (6)
19 Deep pit (6)
20 Palpitate (5)

Across

1 Closing section of music (4)
3 People who act pretentiously (4-4)
9 Person proposed for office (7)
10 ___ Robson: British tennis player (5)
11 County of SE England (5)
12 Simian (7)
13 Knocked gently (6)
15 Number of Apostles (6)
17 Prevented (7)
18 Creative thoughts (5)
20 Epic poem ascribed to Homer (5)
21 Throw into disorder (7)
22 Recently married person (5-3)
23 Small vipers (4)

Down

1 Close mental application (13)
2 Pantomime ___ : comic characters (5)
4 Dog-like mammals (6)
5 Boxing class division (12)
6 Pertaining to a river (7)
7 Brazenness (13)
8 By chance (12)
14 Trailer (7)
16 Advance evidence for (6)
19 Jessica ___-Hill : British heptathlete (5)

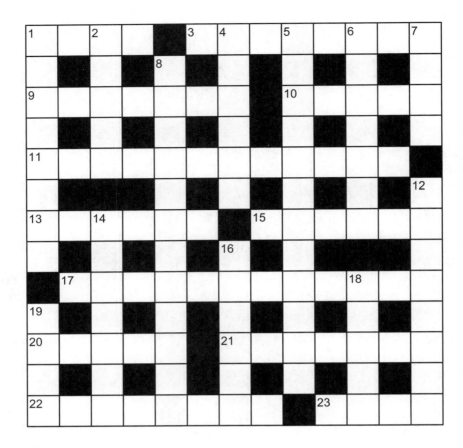

Across

1 Expose to danger (4)
3 Driver of a horse-drawn carriage (8)
9 Nearest (7)
10 Type of tooth (5)
11 Blasphemous (12)
13 What a spider makes (6)
15 Socially awkward (6)
17 Unfriendly (12)
20 Movable joint a door swings on (5)
21 Sincere (7)
22 Examined in detail (8)
23 ___ and wherefores: reasons for something (4)

Down

1 Bag carried on your back (8)
2 Indifferent to emotions (5)
4 Vent (6)
5 Blends; mixtures (12)
6 Soft-bodied invertebrate (7)
7 Standard regarded as typical (4)
8 Intentionally (12)
12 Educators (8)
14 A rich mine; big prize (7)
16 Language (6)
18 Upper part of the leg (5)
19 Ostrich-like bird (4)

No. 26

Across
1 Small boring tool (6)
7 Happened (8)
8 Rocky hill (3)
9 Writing desk (6)
10 Proper (4)
11 Slender plants of the grass family (5)
13 Beginner (7)
15 Trembles (7)
17 Tears (anag) (5)
21 Defer action (4)
22 Those expelled from a country (6)
23 Snow runner (3)
24 Prompted to think of (8)
25 Day of rest (6)

Down
1 Water channel (6)
2 Form of limestone (6)
3 Tall narrow building (5)
4 Frees from a criminal charge (7)
5 Gets ready (8)
6 Arise from (6)
12 Fit together easily (8)
14 Pals (7)
16 Lifted with effort (6)
18 Flipped a coin (6)
19 Give formal consent to (6)
20 Makes fast with ropes (5)

Across

1 Support; help (6)
5 Newt (3)
7 In the company of (5)
8 Arc of coloured light (7)
9 Fruits of the palm (5)
10 Barely adequate (8)
12 In slow time (of music) (6)
14 Very dirty (6)
17 Jubilant (8)
18 Chris ___ : British radio DJ (5)
20 Fatty substance (7)
21 Accustom (5)
22 Intentionally so written (3)
23 Safe place (6)

Down

2 Large marine algae (7)
3 Slower than sound (8)
4 Not hot (4)
5 One absorbed in themselves (7)
6 Day of the week (7)
7 Eg an Oscar or Grammy (5)
11 Aggressive use of force (8)
12 Calls for (7)
13 Living in water (7)
15 Searching for (7)
16 Expulsion from a country (5)
19 Complacent (4)

No. 28

Across

1 Fathers (4)
3 Be wrong about (8)
9 Chemical element with atomic number 33 (7)
10 Take delight in (5)
11 Science of biological processes (12)
13 Large artillery gun (6)
15 Clay ___ : shooting target (6)
17 Unfriendly (12)
20 Imitative of the past (5)
21 Idealistic (7)
22 Putting into practice (8)
23 Give nourishment to (4)

Down

1 Disadvantage (8)
2 Dance club (5)
4 Money received (6)
5 A system of law courts (12)
6 Move apart (7)
7 Sell (anag) (4)
8 Study of human societies (12)
12 Confined as a prisoner (8)
14 Without interruption (3-4)
16 Improvement (6)
18 Inducement (5)
19 Extent of a surface (4)

No. 29

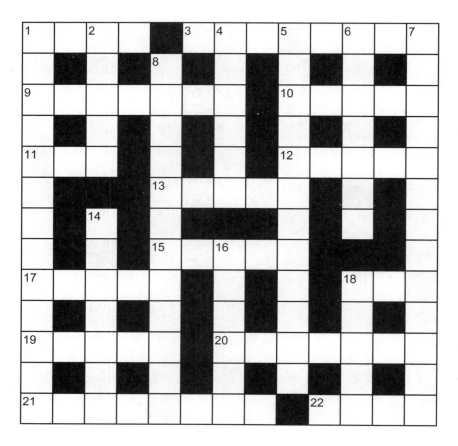

Across

1 Electrically charged particles (4)
3 Last (8)
9 Cushions that support the head (7)
10 Supply with food (5)
11 Sprinted (3)
12 Capital of Ghana (5)
13 Coming after (5)
15 Circle a planet (5)
17 Solid blow (5)
18 Muhammad ___ : boxing legend (3)
19 Organ situated in the skull (5)
20 Sounding a bell (7)
21 Raise one's ___ : show surprise (8)
22 Wet with condensation (4)

Down

1 Very subtle (13)
2 Synthetic fabric (5)
4 Take a firm stand (6)
5 Formal announcements (12)
6 Relating to sight (7)
7 Menacingly (13)
8 Device used to remove a cork (6,6)
14 Bravery (7)
16 Get temporarily (6)
18 Stage whisper (5)

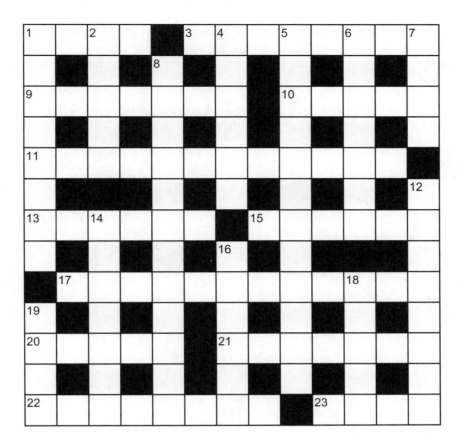

Across

1 Drains of energy (4)

3 Of extreme thinness (of china) (8)

9 Round building (7)

10 In front (5)

11 Skin response to cold weather (5,7)

13 A spell (anag) (6)

15 Roofing material made of straw (6)

17 Version of the blues (6-6)

20 Tiny piece of food (5)

21 ___ May: Prime Minister (7)

22 All people (8)

23 Paul ___ : former England footballer (4)

Down

1 Spread out untidily (8)

2 Paved courtyard (5)

4 Free (6)

5 Marksman (12)

6 Rupert ___ : English actor (7)

7 Outdoor swimming pool (4)

8 Understandably (12)

12 Cord for fastening footwear (8)

14 Make from raw materials (7)

16 Subatomic particle (6)

18 Obtain information from various sources (5)

19 Land measure (4)

Across

1 Meal eaten outdoors (6)
4 Respiratory condition (6)
9 Repository (7)
10 Begged (7)
11 Beguile (5)
12 Scope or extent (5)
14 Decompose (5)
15 What a mycologist studies (5)
17 Ooze (5)
18 Relating to knowledge based on deduction (1,6)
20 Takes small bites (7)
21 State of mental strain (6)
22 Serious situation (6)

Down

1 Flatfish (6)
2 Plant of the primrose family (8)
3 Phrase that is not taken literally (5)
5 At an unspecified future time (7)
6 Clutched (4)
7 Among (6)
8 Expressing disapproval of (11)
13 Rod-shaped bacterium (8)
14 Refuses to acknowledge (7)
15 Go up in ____ : be destroyed by fire (6)
16 As compared to (6)
17 Moderate and well-balanced (5)
19 Lion noise (4)

Across

1 Speed relative to sound (4)
3 Adhering to closely (8)
9 Bring to life (7)
10 Go in (5)
11 Uncomplimentary (12)
13 Wading birds (6)
15 Chase (6)
17 Awkward; untimely (12)
20 Insect larva (5)
21 Nasal opening (7)
22 Physiologically dependent (8)
23 ___ Webb: Welsh rugby player (4)

Down

1 Calculated and careful (8)
2 Precipice (5)
4 A score (6)
5 Happiness (12)
6 Aims or purposes (7)
7 ___ Barlow: Take That singer (4)
8 Extremely harmful (12)
12 Cold-blooded animals (8)
14 Meander (anag) (7)
16 ___ Q: musical (6)
18 Our planet (5)
19 ___ Kournikova: former tennis star (4)

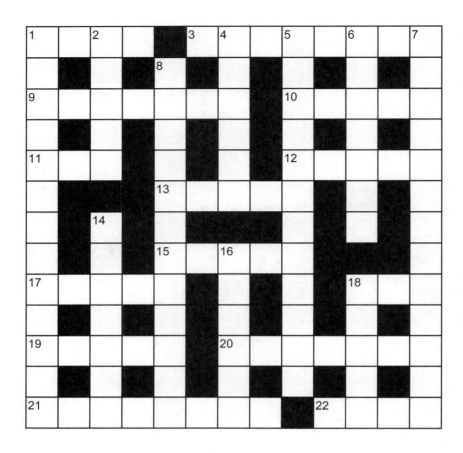

Across
1 Cleanse (4)
3 Friendly (8)
9 Short trips on another's behalf (7)
10 Settle for sleep (of birds) (5)
11 Bruce ___ : martial artist (3)
12 Favouring extreme views (5)
13 Competed in a speed contest (5)
15 Run away with a lover (5)
17 Remnant of a dying fire (5)
18 Popular beverage (3)
19 Unit of light (5)
20 Illness (7)
21 Provided a service (8)
22 Suggestive; lively (4)

Down
1 Scheming person (7-6)
2 Bout of extravagant shopping (5)
4 Adhesive putty (6)
5 Brusque and surly (12)
6 Swollen (7)
7 Wastefully; lavishly (13)
8 Disturbance; act of meddling (12)
14 Egg white (7)
16 One's twilight years (3,3)
18 Eighth Greek letter (5)

Across

1 Unnecessarily forceful (5-6)
9 Push gently (5)
10 Disapproving sound (3)
11 Smallest quantity (5)
12 Move sideways (5)
13 Cuddles up (8)
16 Type of coffee (8)
18 Not suitable (5)
21 Undertaking something (5)
22 Midge ___ : Ultravox musician (3)
23 Large deer (5)
24 Fortified defensive position (6,5)

Down

2 Mistake in printing or writing (7)
3 Year in which wine was produced (7)
4 Nestle together (6)
5 Requirements (5)
6 Receded (5)
7 Distinguished (11)
8 Consideration of the future (11)
14 Design style of the 1920s and 1930s (3,4)
15 Drug that relieves pain (7)
17 Groans (anag) (6)
19 Active cause (5)
20 Speed music is played at (5)

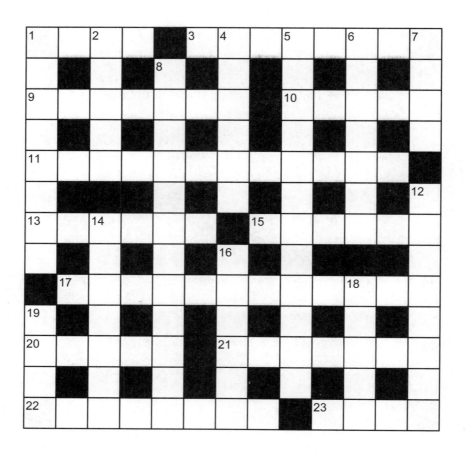

Across

1 Set of playing cards (4)
3 Forest (8)
9 Flotation device in water (7)
10 Feelings and emotions (5)
11 Connection or association (12)
13 Opposite of after (6)
15 Purify then condense (6)
17 Underground (12)
20 Record on tape (5)
21 Suppose to be true (7)
22 North American diving ducks (8)
23 Large deer (pl) (4)

Down

1 Verbal attack (8)
2 Humped ruminant (5)
4 More likely than not (4-2)
5 Tamed (12)
6 Person devoted to love (7)
7 Run quickly (4)
8 Very skilful act (12)
12 Bed covers (8)
14 Set up (7)
16 Three-legged support for a camera (6)
18 Evenly balanced (5)
19 ___ Novello: Welsh composer and actor (4)

Across

1 Printed mistakes (6)
7 Happy ___ : card game (8)
8 Floor covering (3)
9 Uncover (6)
10 Painful or aching (4)
11 ___ MacArthur: sailor (5)
13 Cargo (7)
15 Mix a deck of cards (7)
17 Extreme pain (5)
21 Jelly or culture medium (4)
22 Increase in intensity (4,2)
23 Strong spirit (3)
24 Exclamation of joy (8)
25 Subatomic particle such as a nucleon (6)

Down

1 Fur of a stoat (6)
2 Habitual practice (6)
3 Later (5)
4 Beseech (7)
5 Going red in the face (8)
6 Seek out (6)
12 Confrere (anag) (8)
14 Paradise in Greek mythology (7)
16 Wrangle for a bargain (6)
18 Fish-eating bird of prey (6)
19 Servant in a noble household (6)
20 Skewered meat (5)

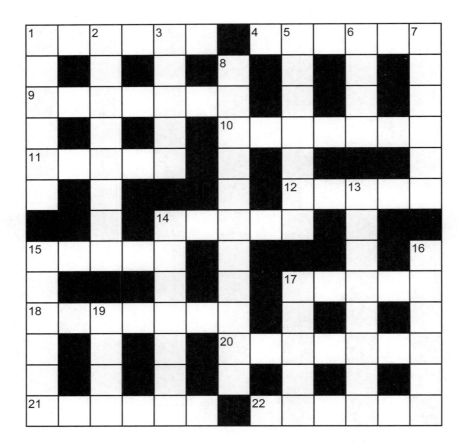

Across

1 Eg Athenians (6)
4 Wagered (6)
9 Break an agreement (7)
10 Venetian boat (7)
11 Female relation (5)
12 Jumps (5)
14 Not dead (5)
15 A gold coin (5)
17 Male bee (5)
18 River of East Africa (7)
20 Remnant (7)
21 Votes into office (6)
22 Subsidiary action (6)

Down

1 Donating (6)
2 Recondite (8)
3 Rogue; scoundrel (5)
5 Sparkle (7)
6 Prefix denoting one thousand (4)
7 Suspends; prevents (6)
8 Discussion aimed at reaching an agreement (11)
13 Relating to trees (8)
14 Non-believer in God (7)
15 Impress deeply (6)
16 Tidily (6)
17 Father (5)
19 Horse and donkey offspring (4)

No. 38

Across

1 Put into action (5,3)
5 Absorbent pad (4)
8 Staple (5)
9 Eg hate or joy (7)
10 Lacking depth (7)
12 Fulfil a desire (7)
14 Had a bad odour (7)
16 Long-lasting and recurrent (7)
18 Saviour (7)
19 Embarrass (5)
20 Trade centre (4)
21 Enthusiasm (8)

Down

1 Young lions (4)
2 Be aggrieved by (6)
3 Sailors of light vessels (9)
4 Anxious (6)
6 Rotates quickly (6)
7 Twining plant (8)
11 Find out (9)
12 Range of colours (8)
13 Pencil rubber (6)
14 Rare (6)
15 Place where something is set (6)
17 Resistance unit (pl) (4)

Across

1 Oven or furnace (4)
3 Diagrams (8)
9 Part of a fortification (7)
10 Soft drinks (US) (5)
11 Remove branches (3)
12 Make a sound expressing pain (5)
13 Big cat (5)
15 Antelope (5)
17 Senior figure in a tribe (5)
18 Fluffy scarf (3)
19 Sandy fawn colour (5)
20 Chanted (7)
21 Prayer service (8)
22 Strategy (4)

Down

1 Intelligent and informed (13)
2 Abatement (5)
4 Gathering up leaves in the garden (6)
5 Person studying after a first degree (12)
6 Not outside (7)
7 Thelma & Louise actress (5,8)
8 Fellowship (12)
14 Hour of going to sleep (7)
16 Something done (6)
18 Hackneyed (5)

Across

1 Striking noisily (8)
5 Revolve around quickly (4)
8 Smooth textile fibre (5)
9 Walks very stealthily (7)
10 Decaying (7)
12 Call together (7)
14 Clogs (7)
16 Instants in time (7)
18 Constantly present (7)
19 Electronic communication (5)
20 Grain (4)
21 Re-evaluate (8)

Down

1 Pavement edge (4)
2 Gas we breathe (6)
3 Female relative (9)
4 A tuner (anag) (6)
6 Financial gain (6)
7 Bouquets (8)
11 Insipid and bland (9)
12 Mountaineers (8)
13 Smear or blur (6)
14 Soul; spirit (6)
15 Infuriate (6)
17 Mountain system in Europe (4)

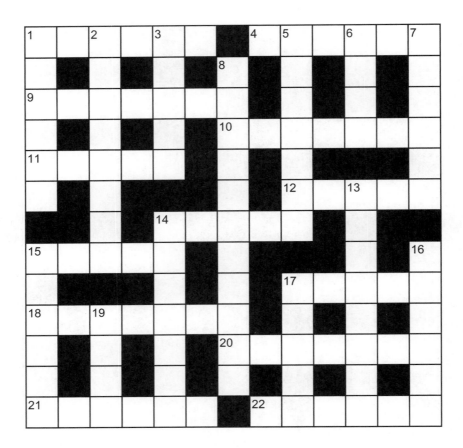

Across

1 Measuring sticks (6)
4 Remains preserved in rock (6)
9 Reindeer (7)
10 Wood cutters (7)
11 Pilfer (5)
12 Indian monetary unit (5)
14 Targeted (5)
15 Pick out; choose (5)
17 City in Tuscany (5)
18 Japanese art of paper folding (7)
20 Wanting (7)
21 Misplace (6)
22 Not awake (6)

Down

1 Remould; allocate parts to different actors (6)
2 Gift of money (8)
3 Insurgent or revolutionary (5)
5 Going away from a place (7)
6 Wise; herb (4)
7 Person to whom a lease is granted (6)
8 Made to order (6-5)
13 Discern (8)
14 Capital of Georgia (US state) (7)
15 Selfishness (6)
16 Terminate a telephone call (4,2)
17 Fastens shut with a key (5)
19 Woes (4)

No. 42

Across

1 Gathering information (4-7)
9 Small firework (5)
10 Bottle top (3)
11 Shed (5)
12 Relating to the kidneys (5)
13 Husband of one's daughter (3-2-3)
16 Inconceivably large (8)
18 Celestial body (5)
21 Relay device (5)
22 Pull at (3)
23 ___ Cooper: US rocker (5)
24 Large fruits with red pulp (11)

Down

2 Squabbling (7)
3 Challenging (7)
4 Tropical American lizard (6)
5 Prohibit (5)
6 Gena Lee ___ : Baywatch actress (5)
7 Tame (11)
8 Youth (11)
14 Rod used in weightlifting (7)
15 Stopping place for a train (7)
17 Chamber of the heart (6)
19 Hot fluid rock (5)
20 Historic nobleman (5)

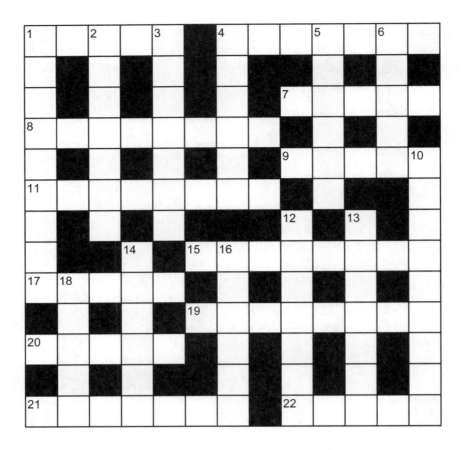

Across

1 Grasp tightly; embrace (5)
4 Collapse violently inwards (7)
7 Become subject to (5)
8 Process of returning to health (8)
9 Curved outwards (of legs) (5)
11 Eg from Montreal (8)
15 Supervisor (8)
17 Piece of information (5)
19 Chord played in rapid succession (8)
20 Put into use (5)
21 Excessive bureaucracy (3,4)
22 Travels by bicycle (5)

Down

1 Put right (9)
2 Leave quickly and in secret (7)
3 Supply (7)
4 Spain and Portugal (6)
5 Long and very narrow (6)
6 Celtic priest (5)
10 Annual compendiums of facts (9)
12 Very low temperature fridge (7)
13 Ruled (7)
14 Naturally illuminated (6)
16 Manly (6)
18 More than enough (5)

Across

1 Sell to the public (6)
7 Protective garments (8)
8 Metal container (3)
9 Subtract (6)
10 Left side of a ship (4)
11 Republic in the Middle East (5)
13 Litter (7)
15 Exceptionally good (7)
17 Horse sound (5)
21 Moves up and down on water (4)
22 Cooks in the oven (6)
23 Former measure of length (3)
24 Decline in activity (8)
25 Having pimples (6)

Down

1 Fully (6)
2 Type of bicycle (6)
3 Water lily (5)
4 Mythical being (7)
5 Tangible (8)
6 Frightens; startles (6)
12 Releasing from a duty (8)
14 Coiffure (7)
16 Quantum of electromagnetic energy (6)
18 Place inside something else (6)
19 Edmond ____ : English astronomer (6)
20 Young deer (pl) (5)

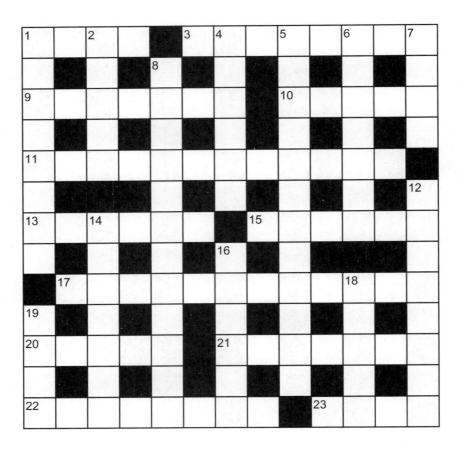

Across

1 ___ grand: type of piano (4)
3 Banister (8)
9 Joined to something (7)
10 Badgers' homes (5)
11 A perfumed liquid (3,2,7)
13 Follows (6)
15 Get away from (6)
17 Upper chamber in Parliament (5,2,5)
20 Speak in public without preparation (2-3)
21 Ennoble (7)
22 Mammal with a spiny coat (8)
23 Push; poke (4)

Down

1 Wristband (8)
2 Small and elegant (5)
4 Writer (6)
5 Very sad (12)
6 Aerial (7)
7 Opposite of win (4)
8 Not capable of justification (12)
12 Add beets (anag) (8)
14 Marred (7)
16 Lively Spanish dance (6)
18 Armature of a generator (5)
19 Uproarious party; hit hard (4)

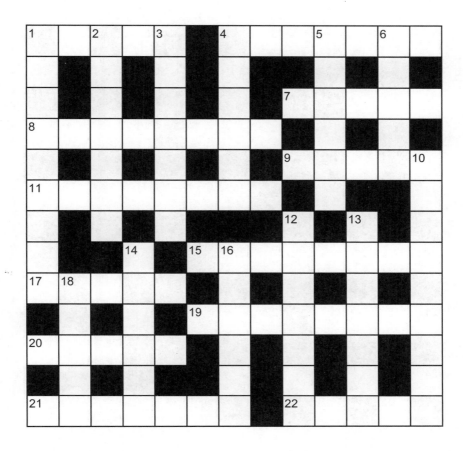

Across

1 Fine-quality coffee (5)
4 Fragmentary (7)
7 Dominant theme (5)
8 Registered (8)
9 Divide by cutting (5)
11 Sledge (8)
15 Light afternoon meal (5,3)
17 Viewpoint or angle (5)
19 Horrified (8)
20 Performed on stage (5)
21 Rider (7)
22 Show indifference with the shoulders (5)

Down

1 Of great significance (9)
2 Winged angelic beings (7)
3 Comparison (7)
4 Representation of a concept; diagram (6)
5 Made amends for (6)
6 Self-respect (5)
10 Concerning (9)
12 Expeditions to observe animals (7)
13 Ben ____ : US comedian and actor (7)
14 Ill (6)
16 Do something again (6)
18 Fortunate (5)

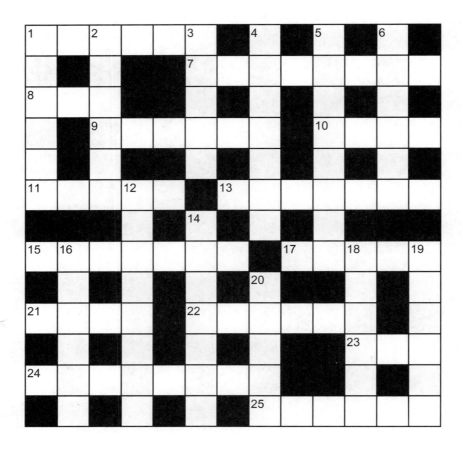

Across

1 Glowing with light (6)
7 Space ___ : arcade game (8)
8 ___ up: consume fully (3)
9 ___ Conan Doyle: author (6)
10 Near (4)
11 Relay (anag) (5)
13 Brave (7)
15 Given generously (7)
17 Local authority rule (2-3)
21 Vein of metal ore (4)
22 Free of an obstruction (6)
23 Cohere (3)
24 Confirm (8)
25 Glass opening in a wall (6)

Down

1 Shrub with glossy leaves (6)
2 Very milky (6)
3 Levy (5)
4 Conquered by force (7)
5 Individuality (8)
6 Fire-breathing monster (6)
12 Relating to critical explanation (8)
14 Not artificial (7)
16 Line of equal pressure on a map (6)
18 Fell behind (6)
19 Wood used for cricket bats (6)
20 Type of small fastener (5)

Across

1 Sink (anag) (4)
3 Stone of great size (8)
9 Tiny sum of money (7)
10 Legal process (5)
11 Gives off (5)
12 Passionate (7)
13 Residential district (6)
15 Punctuation marks (6)
17 Got too big for something (7)
18 Suffuse with colour (5)
20 Printed insert supplied with a CD (5)
21 A very long time ago (4,3)
22 Wrongdoings (8)
23 ___ Khan: British boxer (4)

Down

1 Style of painting (13)
2 Service colour of the army (5)
4 Followed (6)
5 Relating to horoscopes (12)
6 One of the platinum metals (7)
7 Fairground ride (6-7)
8 Short story or poem for children (7,5)
14 Fights (7)
16 Moved back and forth (6)
19 Darken (5)

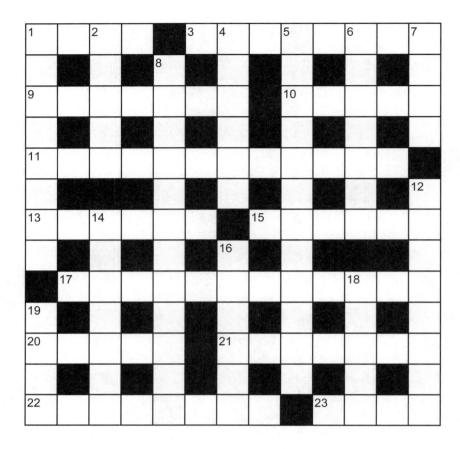

Across

1 Seethe (4)
3 Photograph (8)
9 Instructions on how to cook dishes (7)
10 Monastery church (5)
11 Variety of wildlife in an area (12)
13 Injure (6)
15 Sample of cloth (6)
17 Not capable of reply (12)
20 Stringed instrument (5)
21 Breathed in (7)
22 Plan anew (8)
23 Prophet (4)

Down

1 Portend (8)
2 Very masculine (5)
4 Tensed (anag) (6)
5 Laudatory (12)
6 Natural environment (7)
7 Playthings (4)
8 Scallions (6,6)
12 Device that chops up documents (8)
14 Mixed together (7)
16 Possessing (6)
18 Lump or bump (5)
19 Skin mark from a wound (4)

Across

1 Mean (5-6)
9 Regal (5)
10 Long period of time (3)
11 Rigid (5)
12 Group of eight (5)
13 Sentiments (8)
16 Unable to appreciate music (4-4)
18 Utter repetitively (5)
21 Point in question (5)
22 Slippery fish (3)
23 Images of deities (5)
24 Comprehends (11)

Down

2 Restricted in use (7)
3 Excess (7)
4 Cooking in hot oil (6)
5 Group of shots (5)
6 Upright (5)
7 Discontented (11)
8 Place where fighting occurs (11)
14 ___ Joan Hart: American actress (7)
15 Ate and drank sumptuously (7)
17 Repulsive (6)
19 The lion who rules over Narnia (5)
20 Garbage or drivel (5)

Across

1 Unproven (8)
5 Bone of the forearm (4)
8 Not at all (5)
9 Reserved (7)
10 Food samplers (7)
12 Occupants of a rented property (7)
14 Derived from living matter (7)
16 Angers (7)
18 Letter (7)
19 Gains possession of (5)
20 System of contemplation (4)
21 Allocated (8)

Down

1 Tall vases (4)
2 Inn (6)
3 The showing of a film (9)
4 Proclamations (6)
6 Hired out (6)
7 Uncertain if God exists (8)
11 Type of pasta (9)
12 Felony (8)
13 Weeping (6)
14 Willow twigs (6)
15 Table linen (6)
17 Sued (anag) (4)

No. 52

Across
1 Biochemical catalyst (6)
5 Tree (3)
7 Teams (5)
8 Sterile (7)
9 Crouch (5)
10 Eg resident of Cairo (8)
12 Large snake (6)
14 Where bread is made (6)
17 Anxiousness (8)
18 Restore factory settings (5)
20 Alfresco (7)
21 British noblemen (5)
22 Opposite of no (3)
23 Wrinkle in an item of clothing (6)

Down
2 Flower arrangement (7)
3 Random change (8)
4 Chances of winning (4)
5 Title appended to a man's name (7)
6 Dominion (7)
7 Dispose of (5)
11 Object that gives out heat (8)
12 Scare rigid (7)
13 Long locks of hair (7)
15 Lives in (7)
16 Goodbye (Spanish) (5)
19 Sailors (4)

No. 53

Across

1 Clay pottery (11)
9 Punctuation mark (5)
10 Loud noise (3)
11 Sense of seeing (5)
12 Small heron (5)
13 Wheeled supermarket vehicles (8)
16 Country in Asia (8)
18 With ___ breath: anxiously (5)
21 Prologue (abbrev) (5)
22 Shed tears (3)
23 Small body of land (5)
24 Daring (11)

Down

2 French city (7)
3 Perceived by touch (7)
4 Hostility (6)
5 Large marine mammal (5)
6 Traveller on horseback (5)
7 Transfer responsibility elsewhere (4,3,4)
8 Initiators (11)
14 Catches fire (7)
15 Floating wreckage (7)
17 Stableman (6)
19 Herb (5)
20 Believer in a supreme being (5)

Across
1 Call to mind (4)
3 Moving at speed (8)
9 Most tidy (7)
10 Camera image (abbrev) (5)
11 Kind or sort (3)
12 Exhibited (5)
13 Ciphers (5)
15 Small lakes (5)
17 Confound (5)
18 Four-wheeled road vehicle (3)
19 Gets less difficult (5)
20 Evaded (7)
21 Longing (8)
22 Ancient city (4)

Down
1 In a thoughtful manner (13)
2 Trail (5)
4 Too many to be counted (6)
5 Act of reclamation (12)
6 Form of an element (7)
7 Amiably (4-9)
8 Food shop (12)
14 Salt lake in the Jordan valley (4,3)
16 Recover (6)
18 Type of tree (5)

Across

1 Intentionally hidden (8)
5 Volcano in Sicily (4)
8 Understand (5)
9 Surround entirely (7)
10 Pungent gas (7)
12 Skeleton of a motor vehicle (7)
14 Small house (7)
16 Deciphering machine (7)
18 Intrusions (7)
19 Dietary roughage (5)
20 Deities (4)
21 Recurrent (8)

Down

1 Spur on (4)
2 Emotional shock (6)
3 Restrained (9)
4 Musical dramas (6)
6 Natural skill (6)
7 Hand clapping (8)
11 Powerful; very skilful (9)
12 Hugging (8)
13 Coders (anag) (6)
14 Brusque and irritable (6)
15 Middle Eastern language (6)
17 Ringing instrument (4)

Across

1 Domesticated llama (6)
4 Participant in a game (6)
9 Make less taut (7)
10 Let up (7)
11 Levels; ranks (5)
12 General hatred (5)
14 Throw (5)
15 Ice dwelling (5)
17 Path to follow (5)
18 Playful compositions (7)
20 Driving out (7)
21 Assumes as a fact (6)
22 Young swan (6)

Down

1 Valuable things; strengths (6)
2 Calm and free from strife (8)
3 Baked sweet treats (5)
5 Captain's record (7)
6 ___ bear: ursine cartoon character (4)
7 Restore honour (6)
8 Direction (11)
13 Unwelcome intrusion (8)
14 Morally depraved (7)
15 Arch of the foot (6)
16 Journey by air (6)
17 Petulant (5)
19 Small shelters (4)

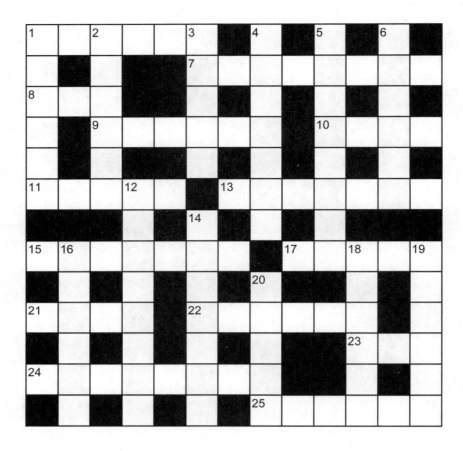

Across

1 Turning armatures (6)
7 Street closed at one end (3-2-3)
8 Used to be (3)
9 Climbs (6)
10 Link a town with another (4)
11 Church farmland (5)
13 Stated the meaning of (7)
15 Into parts (7)
17 Starts to bubble (of liquid) (5)
21 The wise men (4)
22 Country in the Middle East (6)
23 Type of viper (3)
24 Unorthodox person (8)
25 Wears away (6)

Down

1 Arguing (6)
2 Fine cloth; type of paper (6)
3 Skin on top of the head (5)
4 Classic James Joyce novel (7)
5 Neutral particle with negligible mass (8)
6 Grammatical case (6)
12 Blazes seen on 5th November (8)
14 Hairpiece (7)
16 Dung beetle (6)
18 Land surrounded by water (6)
19 Wesley ___ : US actor (6)
20 Male duck (5)

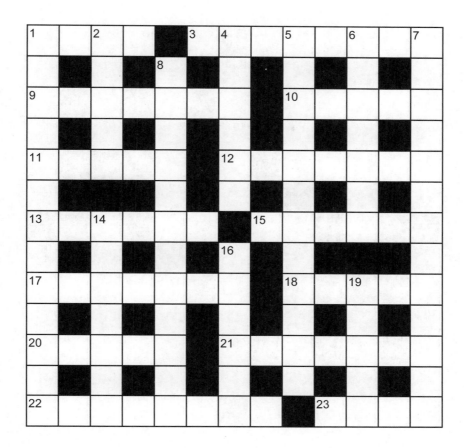

Across
1 Mediocre (2-2)
3 Greek dish (8)
9 Stimulate a reaction (7)
10 Respond to (5)
11 Supply with new weapons (5)
12 Piece of furniture (7)
13 Small pit or cavity (6)
15 Academy Awards (6)
17 Last longer than (7)
18 ___ Klum: supermodel (5)
20 Grasslike marsh plant (5)
21 North Atlantic food fish (7)
22 Christmas season (8)
23 Dairy product (4)

Down
1 In a manner that exceeds what is necessary (13)
2 Minute pore in a leaf (5)
4 US state (6)
5 Atmospheric layer (12)
6 Deficiency of red blood cells (7)
7 Amazingly (13)
8 Beginning (12)
14 Stronghold (7)
16 Curved (6)
19 Nationality of Pierce Brosnan (5)

Across

1 Self-supporting structures (6)
4 Powerful (6)
9 Fear of heights (7)
10 Brother's children (7)
11 Loop with a running knot (5)
12 Consumed (5)
14 Written agreements (5)
15 Levies (5)
17 Sound loudly (5)
18 Geoffrey ___ : English poet (7)
20 Clumsy (7)
21 Tempt (6)
22 Not working (6)

Down

1 Season of the Church year (6)
2 Bodily (8)
3 Select class (5)
5 Places of worship (7)
6 Seep; exude (4)
7 Mel ___ : Braveheart actor (6)
8 Speculative (11)
13 Light axe (8)
14 Able to read minds (7)
15 Equipment for fishing (6)
16 Introduction (4-2)
17 One who makes bread (5)
19 Female relation (4)

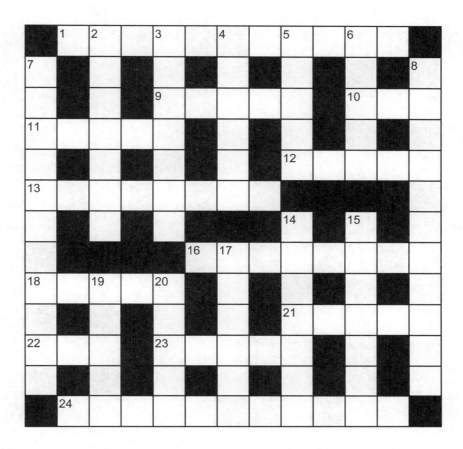

Across

1 The squandering of money (11)
9 Warning noise from an emergency vehicle (5)
10 School of Mahayana Buddhism (3)
11 City in West Yorkshire (5)
12 Core group; basic unit (5)
13 Bedrooms (8)
16 Long foot race (8)
18 Semiaquatic mammal (5)
21 Trite (anag) (5)
22 Female sheep (3)
23 Japanese food (5)
24 Forever (2,9)

Down

2 Momentum (7)
3 Official sitting (7)
4 Young pig raised for food (6)
5 Invigorating medicine (5)
6 Seeped (5)
7 Deliberately cruel (4-7)
8 Free from control (11)
14 Type of vermouth (7)
15 Country house (7)
17 Andre ___ : former tennis player (6)
19 Pattern (5)
20 Ascended (5)

Across
1 Pilfers (6)
5 Mock (3)
7 Loosely-woven cloth (5)
8 Data input device (7)
9 Leaf of a fern (5)
10 Wealthy (8)
12 Former female pupil (6)
14 Recognition (6)
17 Formal speeches (8)
18 Semiconductor (5)
20 Imaginary creature (7)
21 Titled (5)
22 Unhappy (3)
23 Insect that transmits sleeping sickness (6)

Down
2 Considerate; diplomatic (7)
3 Pasta in the form of narrow ribbons (8)
4 Ride the waves (4)
5 Ricochet (7)
6 Unrecoverable money owed (3,4)
7 Crunch; wear down (5)
11 Pointers (anag) (8)
12 Wolfgang ___ Mozart: composer (7)
13 Not attached or tied together (7)
15 Entrails (7)
16 Criminal deception (5)
19 Prestigious TV award (4)

Across

1 Cheap accommodation provider (5,6)
9 Lively Bohemian dance (5)
10 Drowned river valley (3)
11 Covered the inside of a bin (5)
12 Light canoe (5)
13 Opposite of westward (8)
16 Imposing (8)
18 Pastime (5)
21 Excuse of any kind (5)
22 SI unit of illuminance (3)
23 Type of poem (5)
24 Amazing (11)

Down

2 Eccentricity (7)
3 Hierarchical (3-4)
4 Give a loud shout (6)
5 Quick meal (5)
6 Ahead of time (5)
7 Orca (6,5)
8 Travelling with a rucksack (11)
14 Corrupt (7)
15 Inverts (anag) (7)
17 Birthplace of St Francis (6)
19 Crates (5)
20 Loutish person (5)

Solutions

No. 1

```
C A B S   A C A D E M I A
A   E   I   A   I     I S
R E L E N T S   F U S E S
B   L   D   I   F   F   E
O B E S E   N O I S I E R
N     P   G   C   T     T
I S S U E S   M U E S L I
F   H   N   G   L     V
E C U A D O R   T H R E E
R   D   E   O   I   A   N
O G D E N   T R E S T L E
U   E   C   T   S   I   S
S U R V E Y O R   L O G S
```

No. 2

```
U P O N   G A R D E N E R
N   W   C   B   E   U   O
I C I C L E S   M E R Y L
M   N   A   E   O     S L
P I G   I N   N A I V E
E   A     R A T E S   N   R
A   C   V     T   G   C O
C O   O C C U R     O   O
H A N D Y   O   A   P E A
A   C   A     M   B   L S
B J O R N   B E L F A S T
L   C   C   A   E   T   E
E N T R E A T Y   R E A R
```

No. 3

```
  R E A P P R A I S A L
A   X   O   A   N   E   A
N T   P P E R I L   S O B
T U L I P   I   A   O   B
E   O   I   T   W I P E R
C H I M N E Y S   O   B   E
H   T   G   O   O   B   V
A     M I S S O U R I
M A T E R   N   P   R   A
B   R   I   M   R I G H T
E T A   C E A S E   L   E
R   I   C   T   Y   A   D
  A N N I V E R S A R Y
```

No. 4

```
C O T S   A R R O G A N T
O   O   N   A   V   N   A
N A T T E R S   E D G E S
G   E   W   C   R   L   T
R E M I T   A S C R I B E
E   E   L   A   N   L
S A F E S T   G U R G L E
S   U   T   H   T   S
W O R D A G E   I D L E S
O   L   M   N   O   A
M O O R E   R O U T I N E
A   N   N   Y   S   T   S
N E G A T I V E   G Y M S
```

No. 5

```
Y A M S   B R A G G A R T
E   O   A   E   O   U   O
A N G E L U S   L U T O N
R   U   L   T   D   O   E
B E L L I G E R E N C Y
O   M   D   N   U   M
O C C U P Y   G E N E R A
K   O   O   A   N     N
  S H O R T S I G H T E D
G   A   T   P   L   O   A
L I B R A   I N E X A C T
E   I   N   R   S   D   E
E N T I T L E D   B Y E S
```

No. 6

```
J A P A N E S E   G U L F
U   I   A   T   N   R
D R A G S   R E V E R I E
O   Z   H   E     I   E
  Z V   E S C A P E D
R E A L I S T   O   E   M
E     L     N       M
G   A   L   S E T T E E S
U P S W E P T   I   L
L   K   A   N   I   D
A V I D I T Y   U N C L E
T   N   E   A   I   N
E D G E   I D O L A T R Y
```

No. 7

```
S H A N D Y     G   T O M
  A   I   H O R S E   O
S P L U R G E   N   O N
  P   E   R   Y O U N G
M E D I C A T E   O   R
  N   T   Z   B   U   E
E S C H E W   D A M S E L
Q   U   D   S   T   M
U   T   P L A T I N U M
A M B L E   U   E   L
L   A   V   M I N E R A L
L   C H E E P   E   T
Y A K   N   A D O R E S
```

No. 8

```
I M P E L S   L   V   S
T   O     C H E M I S T S
A F T   R   G   E   A
L   I   A G O U T I   W H I M
I   T   T   M   B   I N
C R O W N   I L L N E S S
    E   T   E   G
H E A D W A Y   A S C O T
  L   D   N   S   L   I
M I N I   K U N G F U   N
  J   N E   O   T A G
K A N G A R O O   C   E
  H   S   S   P A T H O S
```

No. 9

```
R O S E T T E S   U T A H
A   T   O   V   H   O
S W E E T   A I L E R O N
P   R   E   D   E   E
  R   E M   E S T U A R Y
T R O O P E D   R   T   B
I   O   A   A   E
N   S L   A U D I B L E
N E W N E S S   E   I
I   A   P   S K S
T O N S U R E   M O I S T
U   K   C   A   N   T   A
S O Y A   S T U N N I N G
```

66

Solutions

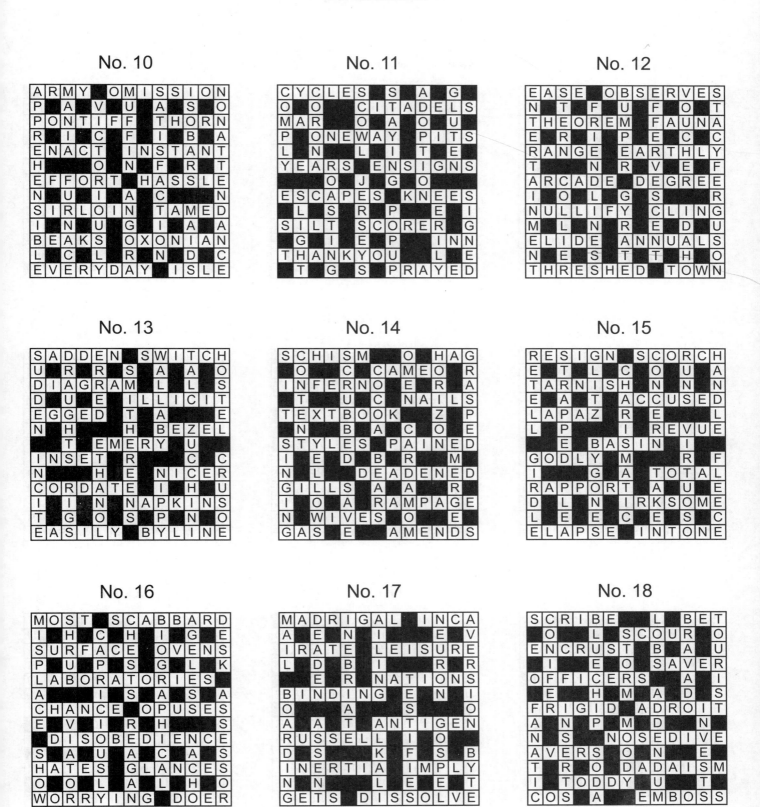

No. 10

No. 11

No. 12

No. 13

No. 14

No. 15

No. 16

No. 17

No. 18

Solutions

No. 19

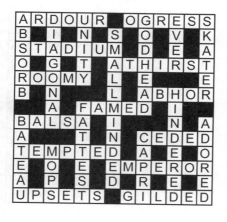

No. 20

No. 21

No. 22
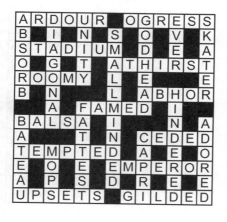

No. 23

No. 24

No. 25
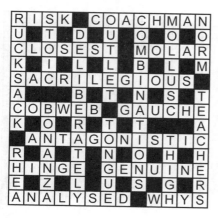

No. 26

No. 27

Solutions

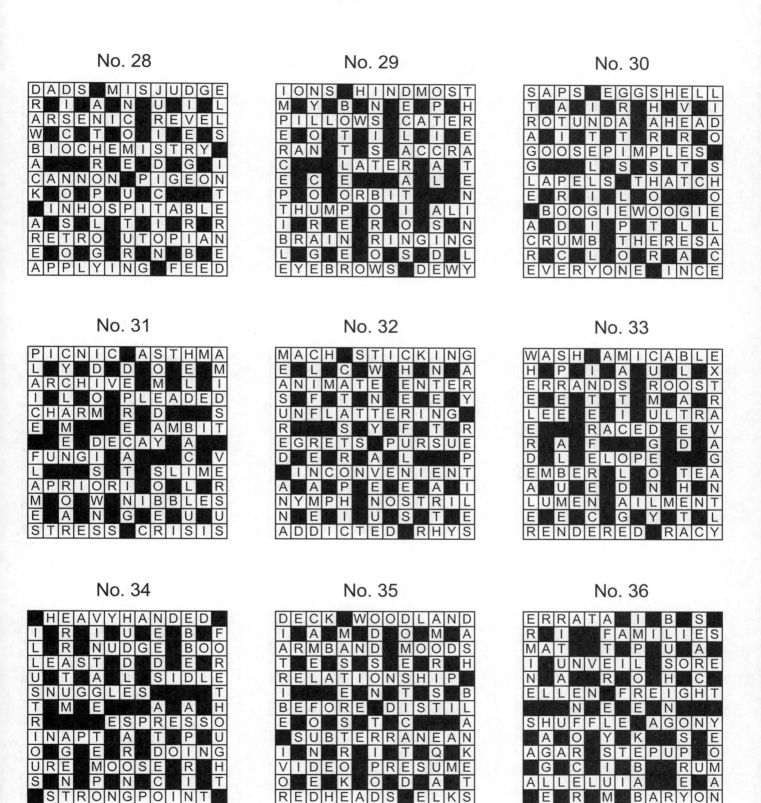

No. 28

No. 29

No. 30

No. 31

No. 32

No. 33

No. 34

No. 35

No. 36

Solutions

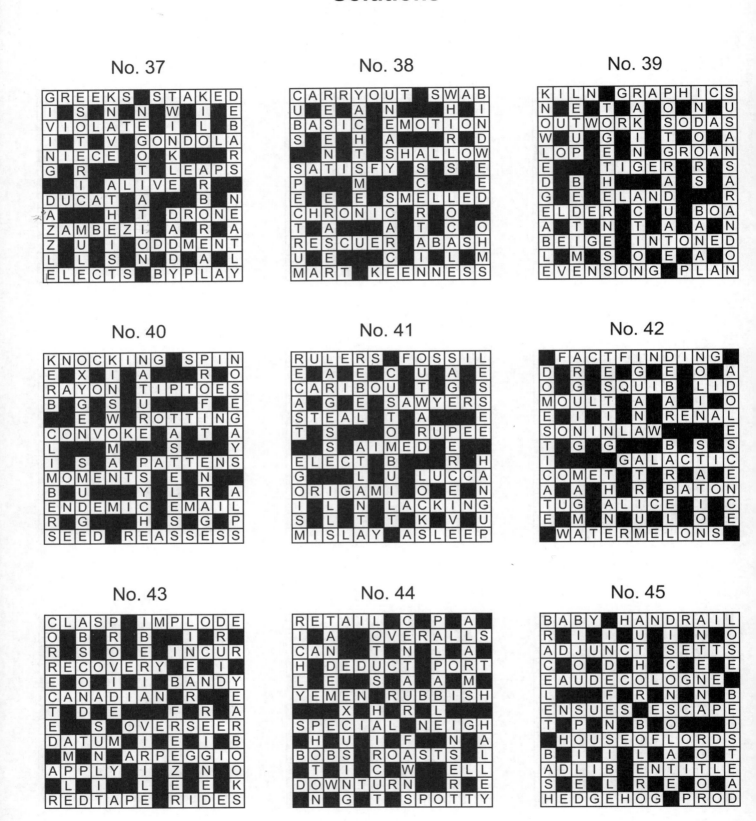

No. 37

No. 38

No. 39

No. 40

No. 41

No. 42

No. 43

No. 44

No. 45

Solutions

No. 46

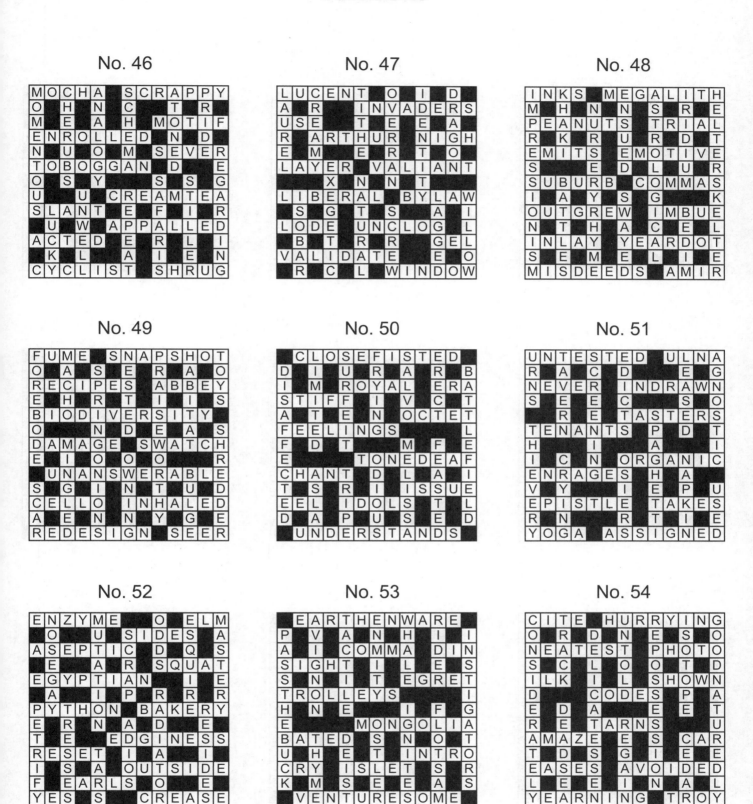

No. 47

No. 48

No. 49

No. 50

No. 51

No. 52

No. 53

No. 54

Solutions

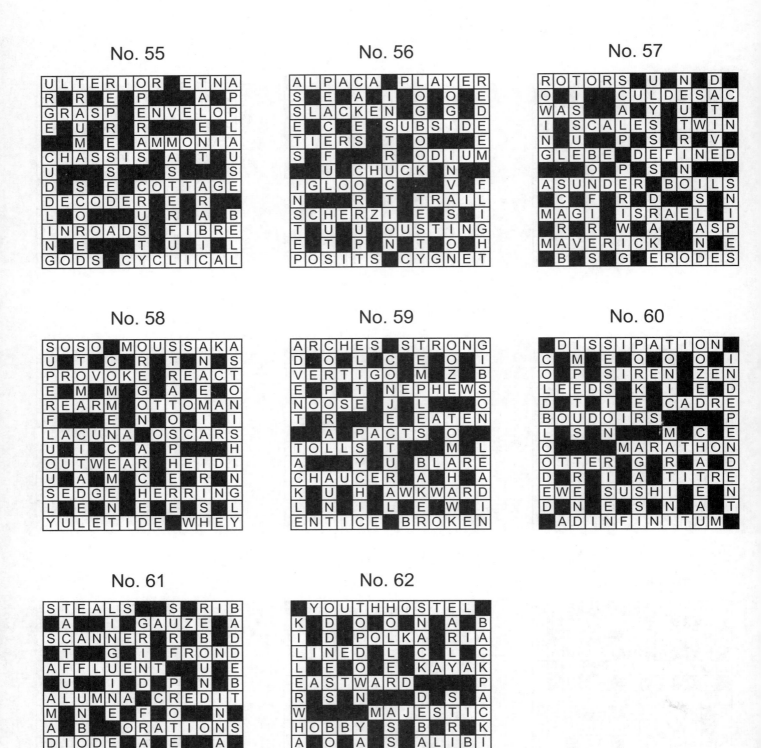

No. 55

No. 56

No. 57

No. 58

No. 59

No. 60

No. 61

No. 62